ON BECOMING A TEACHER

RAUDRA SERIES, AUG '22

JYOTI PRAKASH

Copyright © Jyoti Prakash
All Rights Reserved.

This book has been published with all efforts taken to make the material error-free after the consent of the author. However, the author and the publisher do not assume and hereby disclaim any liability to any party for any loss, damage, or disruption caused by errors or omissions, whether such errors or omissions result from negligence, accident, or any other cause.

While every effort has been made to avoid any mistake or omission, this publication is being sold on the condition and understanding that neither the author nor the publishers or printers would be liable in any manner to any person by reason of any mistake or omission in this publication or for any action taken or omitted to be taken or advice rendered or accepted on the basis of this work. For any defect in printing or binding the publishers will be liable only to replace the defective copy by another copy of this work then available.

To all the teachers whom I have met and not met.

Contents

Preface — *vii*

Acknowledgements — *ix*

Prologue — *xi*

1. My Ship Has A Hole — 1
2. My Ship Shall Sail — 6
3. For Teacher — 10
4. For Student — 17
5. Urban And Sub-urban — 22

About Cover Page — 25

End Note — 27

Get In Touch — 29

Preface

This small work of mine is a little attempt to address my dear generation and subsequent generations. Confidence is a very salty thing – the right amount is adorable, but a little more or less can ruin the entire taste. I can never address my senior generations, for they are well equipped with their own stories and experiences to solve their trouble story.

I don't preach, nor do I want to persuade anyone. I just want to tell my part of story. I am not a good story teller. There have been bigger and better story tellers than me.

The world is too small to be unique. There are high chances of someone else, who would have narrated my story in his or her way. But it is my story in my way.

Every time is new. Some freshness that must still be there in my story must attract someone's lost crust.

Acknowledgements

A teacher is never less than a magician. I will run out of words if I start saying about all the magicians I have ever met. But I categorically thank my mother and father, for being my first magicians. If one taught me reading and writing, the other taught me the necessity of reading and writing.

Prologue

I actually never had thought of writing such a thing. But one thing triggered the spark to write the same. I hope some will agree with me, preparatory phase of anything is always equally exciting as adventurous. Due to the anxiety a lot of things happen, sometimes voluntarily, and sometimes Involuntarily. You step on new things every now and then.

I was studying about Albert Camus. The French philosopher bagged the 1957 Nobel prize in literature. A wrong click landed me on a website that had the list of the nominees for the prize in that year. And one name grabbed my attention. I was actually in a moment of shock for me. But thanks to the anomaly!

We are told about celebrating teacher's day in India as a token of appreciation for Dr. Sarvepalli Radhakrishnan and all teachers in the country. Every speech on teacher's day definitely makes reference to Dr Radhakrishnan. But none of them, that I have witnessed, ever had any mention about Radhakrishnan's 27 nominations for a noble prize – 16 times for Nobel Prize in literature and 11 times for Nobel Peace Prize.

1957, the year Camus was awarded the prize for literature, Dr Radhakrishan was nominated for the Nobel Prize in Literature for the eighth time and fifth time for the Nobel Peace Prize. Such an extraordinary feat! I don't know about others, but this new piece of information about second president of India opened the floodgates of adrenaline in my blood.

I
My Ship Has A Hole

With big dreams in mind, and waking up in morning with none – it can never be more bitter. I was feeling as sad as a kid who ran with a fistful of sand from the shore towards his spot to make a castle, but now has only a few grains left in the petite palms.

What now? I had completed all the possible education officially and the last step awaited for a Ph.D. But 2022 gifted me the post-graduation certificate but not a Ph.D. ticket. I was feeling hopeless.

At a well-judged gap of every half an hour or so, A.M. was texting me, "Are you fine?"

I would reply like a well taught parrot, "Yes, I am. What will happen to me?"

"Are you sure?" she would inquire back.

Yes, I was fine, but no I was not fine. I had to hid, "Of course! It was nothing much of a loss. I am not giving up so easily!" But somewhere deep in me I had actually given up.

The uneasy night had passed. Lying still on bed, I looked around. It must have been eight in the morning; at least the intensity of light entering through the creeks of door said that. My dream of getting into an IIT or NIT for a PH.D. crash-landed the previous day as the latter's selection list displayed on their website.

What could be done now? Nothing? Is it that point where I have to handbrake everything?

Confused and irritated, I went out and completed my daily chores. I just went on walking miles and miles like the sea, but had never paused even for a while to look back where I had left my shore.

With each passing moment, I was getting restless: as if the sun was not ready to sink down the unpleasant vista. The scorpion of regret was stinging me hard. The wound was slowly getting blue! The blueness was spreading throughout my nooks and crannies.

History repeats itself? Is it ever possible that it was the first time I was aimless like the moment? A little concentration made me realise such an incident happened with me, but not long back. Five years back, in 2017! I was aimless then too. Every failure injects hopelessness not into the muscle, nor in the blood but in the nerves. The nerves ache.

☙

The twelfth board results were out. After a thunderous year academically and after several ups and downs in my short relationship with C.P., it was time to face the ultimate result. The result was not expected by me neither by my parents to be good and so it was.

65.4% is what I had scored! I had fallen miserably with mathematics, though I had not failed in the subject. Never in my life till then had I been so much thankful towards practicals. Had there been no practical in biology, chemistry and physics, I was sure to face the first ever compartmental exam of my life.

English had saved me. Almost ninety out of hundred. I can never be more grateful to the subject.

After a session of endless accusations and tears, it was in afternoon that I sat with my parents. I too would have sat with my parents if I had scored good marks, but without the tension that practically was building up gradually. It was one of those moments when I learnt how much dangerous a thing silence is!

"What now?" asked my father. It was actually the question that I was asking me, but that has jumped the boundary of my thoughts and has reached my father's.

"After science stream in twelfth, what is left with such low scores? There is no enough mark to get admitted into any decent college for a bachelor's degree in science stream," said my mother.

I was in no state to respond to any question. Father had not gone to shop that day and that was intensifying things for me.

"Arts?" The stream that no science student wanted to go into, suddenly surfaced in our discussion. I was never prejudiced about any stream, but who wants to join the commoners after being grouped with elites? But is it so? What is so elite about science and so common about arts?

"Is there anything left?" said my mother.

I was taken aback. It was not because of changing stream, but because of what my mother said next. "What will people say now? You changed your stream! Your father and I migrated from village to give you a decent life and you finally ended up doing this? Won't they spit on hearing our name, who with great pomp and pride sent you to a private CBSE school and now are forced to study an Arts subject?" The face filled with helplessness and the eyes full with tears is still fresh. Her words were mercilessly wounding me internally.

I was ready to burst into saying, "It were you who choked my throat and made me swallow that hard pill named mathematics in eleventh. It was you who chose the subjects on my behalf and I have faced in the final exam. It was never me; it was always you," but I restrained me from saying anything. I was in no position for a bargain!

Earlier that afternoon, I had texted C.P. about my marks. She told me her marks. I never had had any sort of jealousy for her. She had scored a little more than me. What had actually hurt me were not her marks, but her choice! Her liberty of not opting mathematics had earned her enough marks (at least more tha me). The stormy year had hit us both hard, but I was in a deeper mangrove than her.

Instantly I could hear my father's words echoing in my ears when I had told him about my choice of skipping mathematics and taking some subject else as an alternative... Then why are you taking science? Leave science! Why will you go to a private school, better that you go to any government college and study arts. People will laugh upon learning that you are studying science without mathematics!

Is really mathematics the soul of science? I don't know if its the soul or not, but I know well mathematics is a subject of brilliance. Not all (including me) are good at it. A good mathematician is one who is as perfect as a locksmith - finding the perfect key to any lock.

By evening a small meeting was arranged with M.R.S sir, who then was my neighbour. It was evening and I was greeted by him into his house. "So, what is the problem?"

My mother said, "Guide him sir. I don't know what will happen now and what to do now? He scored such low marks in the final exams that neither his father nor me expected," while I remained silent. My neck was too weak to keep my head up.

"What is done can never be undone! So, it is better not to think of what has happened. Rather think about what to do next. The online portal for the bachelor's degree will be opening up soon. Fill it up before due date and wait. Wait for your selection call. The reality must be digested and embrace the truth."

I said, "yes sir."

"Don't think of what people will say upon hearing about you doing a degree in English. Your mother told me you are good in English, so why don't you keep that as your core subject? People won't understand what, why, how and where. They are too busy to understand it. You too get busy and ignore what others are saying." He took a brief pause as he looked up at the ceiling.

My mother left, and I was left with sir now. "I have convinced your mother. You need not worry about that! You just set a track and get going."

"Yes sir," I said.

"Do you want to take coaching for JEE or NEET?"

I was in no mood to take a break. I denied instantly, "No sir, I don't want to take any coaching." I already had too much hatred for tutions and enrolling for an advance form of the same would have made me go frenzy.

"This general line is not bad. Your science background will help you in disguise. You will have a different view of everything than others in the class. What others will miss, only you will notice it and what others will notice, you will have different view to it. So don't feel ashamed."

I got up, bowed before him, touched his feet and left.

The following days were turbulent. I already had had a bad year with C.P. and I didn't want that dry patch to spread any further. I knew I was good in English, but I wished to be with her - in her classroom studying her subject of interest. She was adamant about taking zoology and I too wanted the same subject as my core subject. But after a good round of discussion, I finally agreed to settle with English and she would go for zoology.

II

My Ship Shall Sail

It was evening and I thought I should go and meet M.R.S. sir. Only he can row my boat out of this whirlpool of confusions. I rushed to him. It was almost seven in the evening.

The smiling face smiled, but there was a stroke of age in the smile, as if the fine spring has got some rust. It saddened me.

I touched his feet. He pulled a chair for me, "have a seat."

I sat. I felt my smile was faint than his. D.S bhai, his son was nearby and upon hearing me, he showed up. "Sir, I couldn't make it."

"What you couldn't make?"

"Like IIT, NIT too..." words refused to come up.

"Not an issue."

"Sir, should I make changes in my proposal?"

He looked at me, "Changes? What sort of?"

"The topic, sir. Am I being rejected for the topic?"

"It can be and cannot be. Who knows who wants what? So, since there is already an uncertainty in it, why to play a blinder?"

I said, "Do I need to change my way of saying... I mean the way I present myself?"

"If you want to change something then you should bring a bit of change in yourself," D.S bhai said.

I turned to face him.

"You need not worry about certain things. Things will happen."

"But nothing is happening," I said.

"Who said nothing is happening? You were rejected from the viva round?"

I nodded my head.

"So, who said nothing is happening. Rather say things are not happening the way you want. Your rejection is also a happening."

Sir said, "Oh leave it. Son, you need not bother about your selection. One day or other... tomorrow otherwise day after tomorrow you will make it, I know."

"You are young. You completed your postgraduation weeks ago. When did you pass it?" D.B bhai raised his brows.

"Third week of May!" I replied promptly. I feel I still wear the robe of ego and pride of completing graduation with good marks! I thought that good marks were enough to get me through any place. But by the time it was night that day, I concluded, my marks are good, definitely they are good, but not good enough!

"And what time it is now?"

"Third week of June!"

He smiled and said, "Only a month ago J.P.... only a month ago you passed the exams. You are still too fresh and too tender. I am not saying that you are not worthy enough! I have listened everything about you from papa. Don't you remember the last time we talked about your career, I had said that you keep on rowing your boat, someday you will definitely make it to the shores!"

"Yes, you are right. But beware of leg-pulling also," sir said.

D.S bhai followed, "People will pull your legs, that's what they are best at. But need to make your legs strong. Make your every step count. Go into hibernation for a season. For six months don't bother about anything other than your books. Locate yourself first, where you actually are? You can't locate yourself, until and unless you isolate yourself." People are crabs?

Sir was looking at a photo hanging on his wall. "The polite lady you are seeing in the frame is my Ph.D. guide. I must say was. She is in her right place, resting peacefully. I still remember, I day I was awarded my doctorate, she came running and hugged me. She was happier than I was." The sudden change on his face was remarkable. As if an invisible shower of rain had rejuvenated his tired and dull smile.

"She was such a fabulous guide!" D.B. bhai added.

What was so special?

"Now a days, everything is available online. Decades back, when I was guided by her, there were almost no means of communication other than letters! She used to send me to libraries, with recommendation letters. Only if I could just regain my youth, I would have shown you how you can actually exploit the resources around you."

The weather around changed. It was hot, but I wasn't sweating. It was humid, but I wasn't feeling sticky. I was relaxed. He continued, "Many times it would happen so, I would visit the department for visit's sake and she won't be round. I would leave, but the next time we met, she would be ready with her queries. From my health to my studies, she was just my perfect caretaker."

I looked at the photo. Those still eyes were glossy with dreams. And those dreams somehow had spread onto the lips of sir. He was smiling now, remembering his old days. "Whatever I am today is because of her."

"That was the time when everything happened offline. There were the least of keyboards, so everything was happening on pen and paper," added D.B. bhai. "On one side they would be kneading dough and at the same time would be closing eyes to remember if any book or any detail is missed."

"I was always welcomed to her house. Towards the end of my research, I was exhausted and on one such fine occasion, I told her that I won't be able to come and hence I will lessen the frequency of visits."

I could see the dew that was condensing in his eyes, "She said, oh such a little problem. M.R.S why don't you take Sir's scooter? Now-a-days he travels by four-wheeler. Take it and test ride it, if you can control it."

A certain part in me, urged to ask, if he could ride it or not. I think it was my childishness, and I am glad I didn't.

"So, the fact still stays the same. Don't give up! You are young. You have certain plans. So better you back them. Give yourself some time. With time everything will make meaning."

I was ready to leave. I had got my lesson. "There will be teachers who will reject you. But again, there will be teachers who will accept you," he said.

D.B. bhai added, "Those teachers will only accept you, if and only if you don't change your attitude. You went in to the closed room and dared to assert your views on your topic. You dared to show them your potential, so remember you have it. You have that spark." I smiled.

"But..." But? But why but? What but?

He continued, "If you are in a race with donkeys then be one. If you show that you are a horse in donkey's race you will scraped off at the first sight. Wait... learn to be patient! Without patience, nothing happens and with nothing happening you will get nowhere. So, learn where you are, observe where you are."

"Yes, I did learn certain things from interviews."

"This is what I meant when I had said earlier that you have lost only some part, but you have earned a lot as a whole."

I turned to sir, "What shall be my next step then? The same history books, the same theories..."

"Yes! What else should you go through then?"

Recharged, I got back home! And it was my teacher again who saved my boat from self-destruction. Some of you may find my story meaningless. But do remember there is always a place for you. You will always be picked. You will end up in the place where you are!

If sir could find his perfect guide, if time took him to his guide, I know his blessings will guide me to my guide too!

III
For Teacher

As a species, we are brilliant, at least the most sophisticated among all multicellular. But this canvas of brilliance has spread so wild, that we not only do things brilliantly but also ignore things brilliantly. Ignoring things has become an art; unacknowledging things has become an even greater art. How sweetly we do these things!

This little story of mine began when I was probably in the nursery. A little, thumb-sucking boy with eyes full of tears being forced by parents to go to school. I don't even remember if I sucked my thumb or not, nor do I remember if I was crying, but all kindergarten-aged students cry, don't they?

Ah! Is it the only time when the world sees boys crying? I must have been escorted to the classroom by a teacher, who must have bribed my little mind and infant heart with some playful toys or by pointing at some colourful cartoons painted on the walls. And I must have given in.

My little story ends with me leaving my hostel after completion of my post-graduation. The autorickshaw was at a ten minutes distance from picking me and my friend from our respective hostels. And two of my closest friends sat silently in my hostel room. We three spoke nothing, yet that nothingness made more sense than all the delightful moments we have cherished side-by-side.

One of my friends perhaps grew too weak, the arms that once could lift my bulky body with ease were crumbling; two drops of tears ran straight down his cheeks and he removed his glasses to wipe them; my other friend who mostly liked remaining indoors, suddenly woke up to leave the room, removed his spectacles, and wiped his little drops of tears. Alas! The world failed to see boys crying this time.

The auto finally came and they both helped me load my bags and trolleys. They accompanied us to our academic block. We went in to meet our teachers. Four they were, in number. I touched their feet and they expressed their best wishes for me. And I left silently. I had nothing but silence to speak.

My other friend who was traveling with me had her train two and half hours before mine. And by five in the evening, I was all alone. I was left with my phone only. I was staring at my phone and trying to kill my boredom. I was missing her and the empty station was adding flames to it.

A little portion of my life ended in these point two points. In both cases, I was trying to escape. What had I earned in my life? What will I gain in life? Life outside the classroom is a jumbo puzzle. Like the rattle of any rattlesnake I could hear the buzz in my mind due to the confusions.

My story till now is straight, they have two ends and they don't merge. The ends run parallel to each other. But still, they have something in common. I was welcomed by a teacher in the beginning and was blessed by a teacher at the end. I was escorted by a teacher in the beginning and I was wished by a teacher at the end.

Now that I am a week into the mentioned profession, I remember, one of my post-graduation teachers, tall and deep-spoken, texting me "... Just streamline your approach and seek clarity. Best wishes for your new engagement as guest faculty. I see you as a born teacher." (This is just one part of the message and I keep the other part of the text for some other day.)

One of the other teachers, who was instead very young as compared to the former texted, "... Very pleased to hear that you have joined as a teacher, you surely would do justice to it." I have no idea what justice is! But I am glad that at the penultimate step I got teachers who wished me to become like them!

Now that I have stepped newly in this field, I find it new. As a new-born baby who tries to control his/her hands yet ends up scratching his/her face with his/her nails, I find myself newly born. This baby is a week old (as on 12 July, 2022). But this baby teacher stands on the horizon. Beneath me is the time of my studenthood which has flown, but has left behind reflections, and above me lies a vast sky, with endless air and time. I look down, I see what is gone; I look up, I see nothing. I suddenly look at myself and find myself different.

Till that point, I had hardly known what makes one a teacher. How can one ever define a teacher? In fact, how to define? As a painter, who can paint his imagination into the child? As a potter, who can build the best of a structure? Or as a tailor who can take pieces in tits and bits and make something marvellous from anything and everything that is available?

I can hardly keep a count of those innumerable times when I had ignored my teachers, anytime I saw them outside my educational campus. They won't be in their uniform, I won't be in my uniform; they won't be hanging their identity cards on their neck, nor would I have my identity card on my neck; we both would have known each other, yet I won't step up to greet the teacher - two too familiar strangers.

I remember a halt that comes between my short story. I was still a kid then, in second or third grade. With my mother, I was at a fair. I was just awestruck by the number of stalls, by the number of rides. Some of the rides of a towering height. Amidst all these happenings, my mother bumped into my teacher.

The lady teacher was perhaps my class teacher, I had not taken notice of her until my mother made me conscious of her presence. I remember me getting into a state of confusion. I was not in school, should I touch her feet as I usually greet my elders? But what if we both are not on my school premises, she is still my teacher and I am still her student, isn't it? Should I wish her a 'Good Night' (back then I was unaware of the existence of a greeting called 'Good evening')? But before I could realize anything, I had already wished her "Good morning, madam!" What a blunder!

I was in twelfth standard and it was 2016. I don't know what crept into my mind; but whatever it was, it was definitely good! I decided to pull myself out all the private tuitions and back myself up with plenty of self-study. I was left with two primal occupation - School and Self-study.

My plan was simple. What I was targeting for was a long-term result – the finals, but at the cost of my mid-year exams. My score in mathematics fell to 5 out of 100. I was shaken from inside. I had done the inevitable. All my books, notes and the hard work of the entire summer vacation meant a waste to me. I was again put back to private tuitions but this time it was not a group tuition rather individual. The trap I wanted to escape badly instead got me trapped badly.

I always get frenzy when teachers are praised for the success of any student. Is student the only one who seats for the exam? Both work for the exam. One faces the exam physically while the other faces it spectrally. So why one wheel be the one to be praised if the vehicle actually runs on two? It was a question of (my) self-respect, but this in turn exposed me. Was I wrong? Was I right? I don't know.

But what now drives me crazy is the changing time actually have overshadowed the teachers. Billboards of students topping in exams are hung. They are definitely praiseworthy, but are they the only ones to be praised?

If its wrong to fantasize a teacher's prowess over the success of students, is it not an equal ill fantasy to ablaze the town with flexes of student's photo over it without the teachers who actually were behind it? I have heard about times when teachers were the identity of an institution, but now students are the identity. It is not bad. But we need to think - it is good to advertise the students (exclusively) instead of teachers, isn't it?

I remember one strange incident from the maths tuition that I was put into after the tragic score in mathematics. The first class was about matrix. Integration and derivations had never fascinated me. I love them just as concepts and mere words of English. My friends will definitely agree with me on this. Nor did we like permutation and combination.

In fact, probability which was just a venomless snake till tenth, now had grown massive. It no more had the same innocence of the past days. Trigonometry which once upon a time was just limited to some formulae in tenth, now had turned into a beast. Alongside, it had brought its uncles and cousins who were ready to draw blood.

So, long story short, mathematics became that culprit banyan tree who gave shelter to ferocious witches, ghosts and ununderstandable goblins!

This mathematical summarization was not the strangeness that I had witnessed at my tutor's place. He would often go indoors and have some food. After every twenty minutes or so, he would give a sum or two to solve and he would go inside and have something before showing up after ten minutes. What a hunger drive! But that hunger drive was not something very unique to him. The same happens with me. Teaching makes you hungry. Perhaps students feed on the minds of teachers!

I struggled to make it up. Its always tough to recollect shattered pieces. But I passed my twelfth. I had no *flying colours* to soothe me, but at least I had a first class. It won't be a big embarrassment when I would say the marks publicly.

Until a month back, before my appointment I and some of my friends used to discuss how much other teachers earn. Our calculations always ended with a single inference "they just don't earn money, they mint it!"

Ambitions, for a teenagers are like the horns of babirusa which actually tear through its own flesh. The thin line distinguishing ambition and overambition is very often breached. Teachers don't earn out of pity; they earn it out of hard work. It was not until I got into their shoes to teach, I could never understand that they actually spend a lot of energy. I sweat profusely everything I speak. And now I feel ashamed of all the jokes that I once upon a time I used to make upon seeing a teacher sweating. Ah! The days of innocence, ignorance and arrogance!

It's never an easy task - attending the class, neither for the teacher nor for student. I am lazy irrespective of which side I speak for. Waking up early, preparing for the class, being disciplined, and doing everything which makes us less anarchic.

To fault is universal. Both the entities of any successful class can often fault. An ideal teacher is always a student. Without being a student one can never ever be a good teacher. Sponges make the best water soakers. And a perfect teacher is similar to sponge who had soaked enough knowledge during his or her studenthood. But the ability of soaking is just one part, sponge when squeezed gives out every single drop of water that it has soaked.

A classroom is like a jungle. If I describe any class that I have ever been to, I had friends from different levels and different thought processes. Someone would be as fast as a chetah, someone else would be slow as a sea slug, some would be monkeys screeching at the back and some would seat on the front benches with their big, black, bright eyes glued on the teacher and blackboard. Everyone has different needs and everyone is different. In the class ecology, the toppers top the food chain. Everyone fears them!

I am reminded of another short story from my eleventh standard. Actually, it was the spark that broke the barrage of my anger and I decided to leave all the tuitions.

I was sitting with one of my good friends from class, on a hot day. If I am not wrong, it was rainy season and it was humid. I was seating in a class of more than fifty students and away from the ceiling fan. My maths teacher was teaching trigonometry. I had a hard time remembering all the formulae, but I had someone done my homework and remembered some of them.

Sir gave a sum to solve. I clearly remember solving it faster than my friend next to me and out of sheer joy, screamed the answer. My teacher looked at me, gave a grin and nodded. Next to me after half a minute, my friend who was good with mathematics said his answer.

And sir complemented, 'Good! You are right!' But my answer was too the same and I gave the answer before him. So why not me? Any compliment is like air. If given perfectly it will lit a fire, if not it can lit the same fire off. It was there, when my fire went out.

But what I missed that day is that I had lacked a consistency with my performances. A single shower is not enough to quench the thirst of a hot and dry summer.

But the infant teacher in me tells me I am wrong with this inference. Some great man had said the first strike is as important as the last strike to break a piece of iron. Everything starts from zero; night sky welcomes its dear stars one after another.

No matter a student is – a chetah or a monkey, a fish or a snail, nature never betrays anyone with air. All are served air equally.

Humans are like riddles; a student is even more delicate. Mere solving the riddle won't help, the riddle must be understood, observed and encouraged to be more practical. Fancy speeches hardly help unless implemented!

IV
For Student

Being the apex primate, humans know very well to which place they belong and which place they don't belong to. The students are no different and they too have the innate sense of knowing that in the classroom they will be outpowered within no moments. Teacher is the supreme and taking over the supreme is not an easy task.

I remember being in the Scout and Guide in my school days. This upper-hand had earned us the respect and there was less fear for our teachers in us as compared to other. Long live the hierarchy! Eventually, I lost some of that acquired power, for not abiding by the regulation.

Partly due to fear and partly due to respect, the tension is breached. The initiation always ends in a rebel. Being outcasted in the class, who wants it to be? No one is, according to me is born an introvert. Neither an extrovert is ever born. They are made. This engineering happens with the initial interaction with teacher and within the boundaries of a classroom. A teacher should not be a novelty but a norm.

When I was a student on every day that it rained, I wished the school to be called off! If I can recollect effectively, for not more than two days my school was closed for a *Rainy Day*. Ah what a pity!

Both teachers and students enjoy holiday, don't they? It is not just a day off, it is actually an entire day off without any obligations and duties.

But when I used to see teachers coming to school, drenched in rain, with muddy tyres and soaked shoes, I always wondered why do they come actually? Is the pain worthy enough? Is the struggle worthy enough?

Now that I have become one, I too have drenched myself and my shoes. Though I don't wear shoes on rainy days, because when soaked, my digits swell up and they look so eerie to me. They look to me like the rugae as illustrated in my past biology books. Awful!

I feel, certain problems are inherently present in the way we read. The first major problem is the boundary of time! Is it necessary to follow the prescribed time or number of periods for a chapter? Some chapters will be easily accepted and some will of course consume more than prescribed. A mere blame on nature will never solve the problem.

And the topics to be taught – some teachers never like certain topics in particular. How about a situation where it would be the last class to wrap up that ugly chapter and it rains? On one side of the scale, it is to get wet and finish the topic and on the other side it will be to delay the topic for one more day and have another restless night! What would be your call? I personally never had a strong liking for grammar. Grammar for me is that bitter syrup which I had to gulp with eyes shut tight, forcefully stopping the inhalation to avoid the smell, and dropping the syrup right at that point where tongue would feel nothing, as the liquid would flow down to gut. I had to get wet to complete one chapter in grammar so that by the next class I would proceed to some story.

And finally, there is a third reason too. I don't know, if my reason, is vital or not, but it is definitely a reason! Why do we keep doing certain things? To ensure our existence isn't wiped out! Some want to become famous; some want to build a house; some want a vacation; essentially all running after some purpose or other. But purposes don't understand emotions, do they? They demand some material fund. Having a desire won't finance the car to go to the final point! Every day off counts. Every day on counts. Every count is materially guided.

※

At this junction, I feel to address another thing that I had faced as a student. Awkwardness! There is always a generation gap between the teacher and batch of students. A gap means a faultline that can never be crossed with a long jump. A gap means a wooden bridge with rusty nail and shaky foundation. So how to be dependable on each other with such a gap?

Even if we ignore that gap, that status of being a teacher is always highlighted in the class. And a highlight means there will always be a lowlight! With such a high-low dichotomy, teachers enter the class; with such a dichotomy, students enter the class; with such a dichotomy the entire institution runs! But again, this dichotomy is the spine of the institution.

So, what can be done? I believe this dichotomy should never ever be removed, but it must be kept under a veil. Regular classes not only mean disciple, but also it means affection. Regular classes don't only mean strictness, but it actually familiarizes things. The more you see something, the more you accept it. The more you accept it, the more you imbibe it. Ah! Does that not happen in every love story? A mother loving her child, a husband loving his wife, and this would definitely make students fall for their classroom.

The covid times have been shaky. With a sudden shift to online classes, students seating in the comfort of their homes, staring at the blank screen ranting throughout the day – it's an exhaustion! How can someone fall in love with blankness? And in such a situation enforcing students upon doing certain things is a crime. An even bigger crime is expecting them to perform!

Anyone can question my words. And they should. How come a 23-year-old dare to say such things? I can be spoiled brat! I can be anything, but not a perfect teacher. And honestly, I never kept my words as a teacher, all that I have said is what I always wanted to say as a student!

As a student I never loved history, because the way it was written – complex and cryptic sentences. Kings and queen fought and I had to read of them. In fact, some strange king dies in some foreign land and I who has no connection with him is forced to read it. Why? As a student I always felt that vacuum of learning things that I really found pitiable. I pity not for me, but for the books who just were anthologies of information.

Why was I taught mathematics? Why was I taught chemistry? It's not wrong being taught and reading these subjects. Rather the problem lies with the need. What actually was the need of learning all the formulae? Real life never asks formulae, it not only asks but also demands solution.

Will I ever be able to use what you are teaching? This question has always troubled me. Why some theories were rejected while some were accepted? It was until very recently, while learning about literature review and its importance I stumbled upon the answer to my question. We are taught about the past events, about past happening so that either we don't face them or avoid them and act judiciously when are faced with the same.

Ethical ways of living are always appropriated in any civilized society. But the book that actually teaches these are not even taken into consideration. Thin books on moral education are prescribed, but not for senior students. They according to me are the ones who can actually decode the metaphorical meanings.

We want to protect the earth from the invasion of pollution, but we hardly recognize environmental studies as a subject. Either it's a minor subject otherwise if someone opts it for a major subject, the one becomes a laughing stock of not being 'student-enough' because he or she never did take a mainstream subject.

Critiquing a student is easy, but its not easy to be one. I remember one such incident from my tenth class. It was probably a month of back before my board exam. I can't actually recall which subject it was (blame my bad memory).

Me: Why are we reading this?

My friend: Who knows? How does it even matter?

Me: But shouldn't we know why are we reading this?

My friend: Oh! Fool, we are reading this to pass the exams, don't you want to pass the exam?

Me: Just pass the exam?

My friend: Obviously! Read, Pass and Forget!

I felt hollow! I am doing something without knowing what is actually knowing its purpose. This is the point which as a teacher I will avoid. For the few classes that I have taken, I have successfully done it.

Am I blaming the entire culture? No, I can never, nor will ever. Whatever I am, it is because of the blessings of my teachers. But sometimes blessings are bitter too. I am speaking about that bitterness.

The ruined portal that my books gave, aided with the unknown application of the knowledge will always hurt me.

V

Urban and Sub-urban

Sometime in mid-2017...

"Do I have to settle with that degree college?" I asked.

My mother said, "You are just yielding the fruit for the same seed that you sowed." Was she hinting at C.P.? I don't know, and now I don't wish to know either.

"So, I will have to travel by bus?"

"Yes, what else do you think will take you there?"

I said, "I will go for it. There is no chance for autonomous college. The selection process is done." The only autonomous college that I had desired of, was miles away from my reach, though it is only at not more than four kilometres distance from my house.

"Do you know that college you are speaking about is performing fantastically?" said D.S. bhai.

I turned to him. I was wet with sweat. There was no current and only a kerosene lamp kept the place lighted enough to know where who is!

"But..." I was impatient.

"Don't argue J.P. and learn to listen. What is important is not where are you going. It is always important to know why you are going?"

I was listening him speak further, "Maybe when people will listen you are going to a sub-urban place while staying in an urban area, they may laugh. But they forget that something that there is in that sub-urban, is not in urban!"

Current came!

"You need not bother about others. Just remember the students there want to grow. They want to come up the ladder. Always remember to look on the ones who are trying to climb up the ladder, it's their journey which will leave a mark. And there the students are doing it. In addition to that, you will find teachers. Teachers who will aid you, who will polish you up!"

Before leaving, all he said was "Growth always starts from soil. If you see the entire root system is in air, you must conclude that the tree is dead!"

About Cover Page

Some may wonder (if they ever pick this book and go through this section) and find it strange of such a panoramic photo. While most will try to find a photo that can maintain equilibrium with the theme and topic, I have not done it. From my title, most have made it obvious that it must be something about teachership. But I will like to clear this, at least from my side that, being a student is always a part and parcel of being a teacher.

And this transition from a student to teacher must be a smooth one. Any transition brings about new life. With the coming of sun in the morning, a new life rises and with the going of the sun, a different life takes over the central stage. The sun thus brings changes with it. These changes and transitions for me are as equal as I became a teacher from a student.

The cover page represents my smooth transition. As a promise to self, very ambitiously I declare that the ambiguity that I had faced as a student won't find its place with me as a teacher. As a teacher I won't be a boss, but a leader, like the sun, who will give both day to my students to work hard and night for them to relax so they don't burn themselves out more.

End Note

I am deliberately trying to skip certain parts. I believe I will talk about my experiences with him sometime in future. The notion of good and bad teacher and good and bad student is immortal as well as ever-changing. But I consider it is we who define both good and bad - we add meanings and we deduce meanings. And I don't want to judge a case which I would advocate!

I can never be enough thankful to K.K.S Women's college, Balasore, for giving me an opportunity to discover the hidden teacher in me.

I don't even know why I am in this profession. I don't even know if this is my profession or not. In fact, I do not know whether I chose this profession or this profession chose me. But, since I am here, I will maintain my honesty and dedication towards the profession till the time I am here.

Get In Touch

Facebook - Raudra Series
Instagram - raudra.series
E-Mail - raudra.series@gmail.com

www.ingramcontent.com/pod-product-compliance
Lightning Source LLC
LaVergne TN
LVHW092101060526
838201LV00047B/1515